YOU MUST REMEMBER THIS

1944

MILESTONES, MEMORIES,
TRIVIA AND FACTS, NEWS EVENTS,
PROMINENT PERSONALITIES &
SPORTS HIGHLIGHTS OF THE YEAR

TO : _____

FROM : _____

MESSAGE : _____

_____

_____

selected and researched
by
betsy dexter

WARNER 🔵 TREASURES™

PUBLISHED BY WARNER BOOKS

A TIME WARNER COMPANY

Warner Books, Inc.
1271 Avenue of the Americas
New York, New York 10020

Warner Treasures is a
trademark of Warner Books, Inc.

A Time Warner Company

DESIGN:
CAROL BOKUNIEWICZ DESIGN
PRINTED IN SINGAPORE
FIRST PRINTING : SEPTEMBER 1995
10 9 8 7 6 5 4 3 2 1
ISBN: 0-446-91077-5

AT THE BATTLE OF THE BULGE, **GENERAL GEORGE PATTON** SWEPT THROUGH NORTHERN FRANCE, CROSSING THE RHINE INTO SOUTHERN GERMANY.

1944

D-DAY on June 6, U.S. troops established beachheads at Utah Beach and Omaha Beach during the Allied invasion of Western Europe

In Chicago, troops seized the Montgomery Ward department store for rejecting FDR's order to extend the workers' union contract. CEO Sewell Avery was physically removed from his office.

newsreel

HIS WAS THE YEAR AMERICAN FORCES MADE THEIR

NAL THRUST TOWARD VICTORY IN WORLD WAR II.

ECLARING "I HAVE AS LITTLE RIGHT AS A SOLDIER

O LEAVE HIS POSITION ON THE LINE," PRESIDENT

RANKLIN D. ROOSEVELT WAS REELECTED TO AN

NPRECEDENTED 4TH TERM IN OFFICE, ALONG WITH

CE PRESIDENT HARRY S TRUMAN.

AT THE DUMBARTON OAKS CONFERENCE, DELEGATES FROM THE U.S., THE USSR, AND THE BRITISH COMMONWEALTH PROPOSED A PERMANENT INTERNATIONAL PEACE ORGANIZATION, TO BE CALLED THE

UNITED NATIONS

international

headlines

A SMALL GROUP OF GERMAN OFFICERS MADE AN UNSUCCESSFUL ATTEMPT TO ASSASSINATE HITLER

Nazis in Hungary began rounding up Jews and sending them to Auschwitz in preparation for the Russian attack. Addressing the Jewish Council in Budapest, Adolf Eichmann declared: "You don't know who I am? I am a butcher thirsty for blood."

5

EXCEPT FOR CHOICE CUTS OF BEEF AND STEAK, MEAT RATIONING ENDED.

The Declaration of Independence, shipped away from Washington, D.C., for safekeeping in December 1941, was returned and put on display at the Library of Congress.

THE NOBEL PEACE PRIZE WAS AWARDED TO THE INTERNATIONAL RED CROSS.

Playwright Mary Chase published *Harvey*, about a man who liked to drink and his imaginary companion, a giant rabbit.

cultural
milestones

Aaron Copland composed the music to the modern dance piece titled *Appalachian Spring*, at the request of the choreographer **Martha Graham**

radio

Champion of Champions **Bob Hope**

Outstanding New Star **Alan Young**

Comedian **Bob Hope**

Comedienne **Joan Davis**

Master of Ceremonies **Bing Crosby**

Comedy Show **Bob Hope**

Male Vocalist **Bing Crosby**

Female Vocalist **Dinah Shore**

Dance Band **Guy Lombardo**

Program for Children **"Let's Pretend"**

Dramatic Show **"Lux Radio Theatre"**

Daytime Serial **"Breakfast at Sardi's"**

Quiz Show **"Information Please"**

THE POPULAR RADIO SHOW "THE ADVENTURES OF OZZIE AND HARRIET," STARRING OZZIE AND HARRIET NELSON, DEBUTED THIS YEAR.

8

CBS reopened its studios on May 5 with the premiere of "CBS Television News."

television

On May 25, NBC was involved in the first instance of television censorship. Eddie Cantor was in the middle of a duet with Nora Mortan, on **"We're Having a Baby, My Baby and Me,"** when the sound was cut off. The song was considered too "suggestive." As Cantor did his comic hula dance, the cameraman was ordered to change the focus to a soft blur.

science

Quinine, used to ward off malaria, was synthesized by Harvard's Robert Woodward, known to colleagues as the Father of Modern Organic Synthesis.

NEW YORK HOSPITAL, IN NEW YORK CITY, ESTABLISHED THE FIRST EYE BANK, DESIGNED TO STORE HUMAN CORNEAS LATER TRANSPLANTED TO RESTORE SIGHT IN CERTAIN KINDS OF BLINDNESS.

Edvard Munch,
artist and founder of Expressionism best known for his disturbing work *The Scream*, died outside Oslo, on January 23. He was 80.

Wendell Willkie,
Republican leader and presidential candidate, died on October 8, at 52.

Piet Mondrian,
Dutch painter whose neo-plasticism featured primary colors and right angles, died at 71 in New York on February 1.

Antoine de Saint-Exupéry,
French pilot and writer best known for *The Little Prince*, died on July 31 when his plane disappeared on maneuvers over Corsica. He was 44.

milestones

notable births

AURENCE J. KIRSHBAUM,
FO and President of Warner Books, in icago, May 23.

OGER DALTREY,
ad singer of The Who, London, March 1.

IANA ROSS,
ıger and ex-Supreme, Detroit, March 26.

EORGE LUCAS,
ector of *Star Wars*, Modesto, CA, May 14.

AQUELINE BISSET,
tress, Weybridge, England, September 13.

ICHAEL DOUGLAS,
tor, New Brunswick, NJ, September 25.

ARRY WHITE,
ıger, Galveston, TX, September 12.

11

❶ rum and coca-cola The Andrews Sisters with Vic Schoen and His Orchestra

❷ don't fence me in Bing Crosby with the Andrews Sisters and Vic Schoen and His Orchestra

❸ into each life some rain must fall Ella Fitzgerald and the Ink Spots

❹ is you is, or is you ain't, my baby Louis Jordan and His Tympany Five

❺ cocktails for two Spike Jones and His City Slickers

'44

Singer Yves Montand made his singing debut on February 18 in a Paris music hall

hit music

THE ANDREWS SISTERS

12

SPIKE JONES

fiction

1. **the robe**
   lloyd c. douglas

2. **strange fruit**
   lillian smith

3. **a tree grows
   in brooklyn**
   betty smith

4. **forever amber**
   kathleen winsor

5. **the razor's edge**
   w. somerset maugham

6. **the green years**
   a.j. cronin

7. **leave her to heaven**
   ben ames williams

8. **green dolphin street**
   elizabeth goudge

9. **a bell for adano**
   john hersey

10. **the apostle**
    sholem asch

It was a banner year for modern poetry. Robert Lowell published *Land of Unlikeness*, his first book of poems. T. S. Eliot published his masterpiece titled *Four Quartets*.

books

Colette published her novel *Gigi.*

the green bay packers

won the National Football title for the 6th time, tying the record set by the Chicago Bears the previous year for number of titles held by a single team.

In baseball, the **St. Louis Cardinals** defeated the **St. Louis Browns,** 4 games to 2, to take the World Series.

IN HORSE RACING, JOCKEY C. MCCREARY RODE PENSIVE TO A KENTUCKY DERBY VICTORY.

UTAH BEAT DARTMOUTH, 42-40, TO BECOME THE NCAA BASKETBALL CHAMPIONS.

sports

In the Rose Bowl, the University of Southern California blanked the University of Washington, 29 to 0. This marked the first meeting between two Pacific Coast Conference teams in this postseason classic.

In Stanley Cup action, the Montreal Canadiens defeated Chicago in 4 straight games.

44

17

Young **Elizabeth Taylor** co-starred with **Mickey Rooney** and a horse in *National Velvet.*

Paramount's ***Going My Way*** won Best Picture and was produced by Leo McCarey. **Bing Crosby** won Best Actor Oscar for *Going My Way.* Best Supporting Actor went to **Barry Fitzgerald,** also for *Going My Way.* **Ingrid Bergman** was named Best Actress for *Gaslight.* **Ethel Barrymore** won Best Supporting Actress for *None But The Lonely Heart.* Additional awards were given to **Lamar Trotti** for best Original Screenplay for *Wilson* and to **Frank Butler** and **Frank Cavett** for Best Adapted Screenplay for *Going My Way.*

TOP MONEYMAKING FILMS

1. *Going My Way,* $6,500,000
2. *Meet Me in St. Louis,* $5,132,000
3. *Since You Went Away,* $4,924,756
4. *Thirty Seconds Over Tokyo,* $4,471,080
5. *The White Cliffs of Dover,* $4,045,250

movies

The basic gas ration was reduced to 2 gallons a week.

In September, the Office of War Information revealed that passenger cars were being scrapped at a rate of 4,000 a day.

1944 wheels

SAVE STEPS, TIME and TIRE

Willys-Overland announced plans to produce a civilian version of the Jeep after the war.

CLEAN REST ROOMS

BRICK'S

OFFICIAL INSPECTION
TIRES
FOR
RATIONING

PRESTONE
ANTI-FREEZE
2.65

ROSEGARDEN
APARTMENT
3 Rooms - Bat

fashion

BY THE END OF 1944, WITH VICTORY IN THE AIR, CLOTHING — ESPECIALLY EVENING WEAR — BECAME LESS AND LESS SOMBER.

American women had a love affair with the "little cotton dress." This now had a slim rather than dirndl skirt for summer.

Skirts began to be less severe. Waists became more accentuated and tops were figure-fitting.

shopping spree

All-wool high-nap fleece overcoat **$44.75**

Botany pure wool flannel robe **$15.95**

Boy's 2-piece snowsuit **$19.95**

Belts and braces (suspenders) **$5.00**

A SIGNIFICANT BREAK WITH TRADITION, BRITISH WOMEN BEGAN TO WEAR TROUSERS DUE TO THE RESTRICTIONS ON STOCKINGS. IT BECAME A FASHION TREND THAT SPREAD WORLDWIDE. AMERICAN WOMEN WERE SOON WEARING SHORTS AND TROUSERS.

Seventeen magazine began publication. Publishing mogul Walter H. Annenberg started the periodical to serve the **post-adolescent, pre-adult female market.**

final factoid

seventeen

September 1944
5 Cents

Young fashions & beauty, movies & music, ideas & people

credits

archive photos: inside front cover,
pages 1, 9,10, 11, 15, 20, 21, 23, inside back cover.

associated press: pages 2, 3, 5, 6, 16.

photofest: pages 7, 8, 12, 13, 18, 19.

magazine photograph:
courtesy of seventeen

photo research:
alice albert

coordination:
rustyn birch

design:
carol bokuniewicz design
ginger krantz

'44